A FOURTH POETRY BOOK

compiled by John Foster

illustrated by
Peter Benton
Noel Connor
Allan Curless
Arthur Robins
Martin White

Oxford University Press

Oxford University Press, Walton Street, Oxford OX2 6DP

Oxford New York Toronto
Delhi Bombay Calcutta Madras Karachi
Petaling Jaya Singapore Hong Kong Tokyo
Nairobi Dar es Salaam Cape Town
Melbourne Auckland

and associated companies in
Berlin Ibadan

Oxford is a trade mark of Oxford University Press

First published 1982
Reprinted 1983, 1984, 1985 (twice), 1987, 1988

ISBN 0 19 918151 9 (paperback)
ISBN 0 19 918152 7 (hardback)

Acknowledgements

The publishers would like to thank the following for permission to reproduce photographs:

A. Anholt-White, pp. 17, 97; Suzanne Arms/Jeroboam Inc., p. 39; Barnaby's Picture Library, pp. 7, 22–23, 46–47, 50–51, 58, 62–63, 94–95; Peter Brookes, p. 79; Robin Crofts, pp. 114–115; Fay Godwin, pp. 102–103; Keystone Press Agency, pp. 110–111; Frank W. Lane, p. 29; Oxford Scientific Films, pp. 48–49; M. Restieaux, p. 120 (bottom); M. Riegler, pp. 120–121; Vision International, pp. 52–53.
For text acknowledgements see pp. 126–127.

also in this series:
A Very First Poetry Book
A First Poetry Book
A Second Poetry Book
A Third Poetry Book
A Fourth Poetry Book
A Fifth Poetry Book
A Scottish Poetry Book
A Second Scottish Poetry Book

Another First Poetry Book
Another Second Poetry Book
Another Third Poetry Book
Another Fourth Poetry Book
Another Fifth Poetry Book

Phototypeset by Western Printing Services Ltd
Printed in Hong Kong

Contents

How I See It

Some say the world's
A hopeless case:
A speck of dust
In all that space.
It's certainly
A scruffy place.
Just one hope
For the human race
That I can see:
Me. I'm
ACE!

Kit Wright

The Rebel Child

Most days when I
Go off to school
I'm perfectly contented
To follow the rule,

Enjoy my history,
My music, my sums,
Feel a little sorry
When home time comes.

But on blowabout mornings
When clouds are wild
And the weather in a tumult –
I'm a rebel child.

I sit quite calmly,
My face at rest,
Seem quite peaceable,
Behave my best;

But deep inside me
I'm wild as a cloud,
Glad the sky is thrown about
Glad the storm's loud!

And when school's over
And I'm out at last,
I'll laugh in the rain,
Hold my face to the blast,

Be free as the weather,
Bellow and shout
As I run through all the puddles –
'School's out! School's out!'

Leslie Norris

8

Distracted the mother said to her boy

Distracted the mother said to her boy
'Do you try to upset and perplex and annoy?
Now, give me four reasons – and don't play the fool –
Why you shouldn't get up and get ready for school.'

Her son replied slowly, 'Well, mother, you see,
I can't stand the teachers and they detest me;
And there isn't a boy or a girl in the place
That I like or, in turn, that delights in my face.'

'And I'll give you two reasons,' she said, 'Why you ought
Get yourself off to school before you get caught;
Because, first, you are forty and, next, you young fool,
It's your job to be there.
You're the head of the school.'

Gregory Harrison

Playing Truant

Davy
was no fan
of the School Attendance man

Maybe
canes and schools
aren't really suitable for fools

the Law
still demanded
that school should be attended

what's more
the Headmaster
proclaimed him a disaster

being no
great bookworm
his liking for lessons was lukewarm

even so he was fluent
in the art of playing truant

Raymond Wilson

Animal Chatter

a piece of doggerel

The other morning, feeling dog-tired, I was walking sluggishly to school,
When I happened upon two girls I know – who were busy playing the
fool.
They were monkeying about, having a fight –
But all that they said didn't sound quite right.
'You're batty, you are – and you're catty too.'
'That's better than being ratty, you peevish shrew!'
'Don't be so waspish!' 'Don't be such a pig!'
'Look who's getting cocky – your head's too big!'
'You silly goose! Let me have my say!'
'Why should I, you elephantine popinjay?!'
I stopped, I looked, I listened – and I had to laugh
Because I realised then, of course, it's never the cow or the calf
That behave in this bovine way.
It's mulish humans like those girls I met the other day.
You may think I'm too dogged, but something fishy's going on –
The way we beastly people speak of animals is definitely wrong.
Crabs are rarely crabby and mice are never mousey
(And I believe all lice deny that they are lousy).
You know, if I wasn't so sheepish and if I had my way
I'd report the English language to the RSPCA.

Gyles Brandreth

11

Arithmetic

Arithmetic is where numbers fly like pigeons in and out of your head.

Arithmetic tells you how many you lose or win if you know how many you had before you lost or won.

Arithmetic is seven eleven all good children go to heaven – or five six bundle of sticks.

Arithmetic is numbers you squeeze from your head to your hand to your pencil to your paper till you get the answer.

Arithmetic is where the answer is right and everything is nice and you can look out of the window and see the blue sky – or the answer is wrong and you have to start all over again and try again and see how it comes out this time.

If you take a number and double it and double it again and then double it a few more times, the number gets bigger and bigger and goes higher and higher and only arithmetic can tell you what the number is when you decide to quit doubling.

Arithmetic is where you have to multiply – and you carry the multiplication table in your head and hope you won't lose it.

If you have two animal crackers, one good and one bad, and you eat one and a striped zebra with streaks all over him eats the other, how many animal crackers will you have if somebody offers you five six seven and you say No no no and you say Nay nay nay and you say Nix nix nix?

If you ask your mother for one fried egg for breakfast and she gives you two fried eggs and you eat both of them, who is better in arithmetic, you or your mother?

Carl Sandburg

The National Union of Children

NUC has just passed a weighty resolution:
'Unless all parents raise our rate of pay
This action will be taken by our members
(The resolution comes in force today):–

'Noses will not be blown (sniffs are in order),
Bedtime will get preposterously late,
Ice-cream and crisps will be consumed for breakfast,
Unwanted cabbage left upon the plate,

'Earholes and finger-nails can't be inspected,
Overtime (known as homework) won't be worked,
Reports from school will all say "Could do better",
Putting bricks back in boxes may be shirked.'

Roy Fuller

The National Association of Parents

Of course, NAP's answer quickly was forthcoming
(It was a matter of emergency),
It issued to the Press the following statement
(Its Secretary appeared upon TV):–

'True that the so-called Saturday allowance
Hasn't kept pace with prices in the shops,
But neither have, alas, parental wages;
NUC's claim would ruin kind, hard-working pops.

'Therefore, unless that claim is now abandoned,
Strike action for us, too, is what remains;
In planning for the which we are in process
Of issuing, to all our members, canes.'

Roy Fuller

The ABC

'Twas midnight in the schoolroom
And every desk was shut,
When suddenly from the alphabet
Was heard a loud 'Tut-tut!'

Said A to B, 'I don't like C;
His manners are a lack.
For all I ever see of C
Is a semi-circular back!'

'I disagree,' said D to B,
'I've never found C so.
From where I stand, he seems to be
An uncompleted O.'

C was vexed, 'I'm much perplexed,
You criticize my shape.
I'm made like that, to help spell Cat
And Cow and Cool and Cape.'

'He's right,' said E; said F, 'Whoopee!'
Said G, ''Ip, 'ip, 'ooray!'
'You're dropping me,' roared H to G.
'Don't do it please I pray!'

'Out of my way,' LL said to K.
'I'll make poor I look ILL.'
To stop this stunt, J stood in front,
And presto! ILL was JILL.

'U know,' said V, 'that W
Is twice the age of me,
For as a Roman V is five
I'm half as young as he.'

X and Y yawned sleepily,
'Look at the time!' they said.
'Let's all get off to beddy byes.'
They did, then, 'Z-z-z.'

or, alternative last verse

X and Y yawned sleepily,
'Look at the time!' they said.
They all jumped in to beddy byes
And the last one in was Z!

Spike Milligan

16

17

Night Without Light

When the owl cries out
And the creatures shout
  At night
We begin to doubt . . .
Can they see without
  Their sight?

Can they see through black
While we make a track
  Through chance?
Where is front and back?
What was that sharp crack?
  Whose glance?

Who is coming near?
Why this rising fear
  In me?
It is almost clear!
It is almost here!
  I see!

Alan Bold

Moth

Drawn by the eyeless glitter of a lamp
A slickwinged silver moth got in
My midnight study and ran quick
Around the switches of a radio.

Antennae searched the compact powerpacks
And built-in aerials, feet on metal paused
At words like METER-SELECT, MINIMUM-MAX
TUNER, VOLUME, TONE –
Licked up shortwave stations onto neat
Click-buttons with precision feet.

Unable to let go the next examination
My own small private moth seemed all
Transistor-drunk on fellow-feeling,
A voluptuous discovery pulled
From some far bigger life.

A thin and minuscule antenna
Felt memory back-threading as it crawled
Familiar mechanism, remembering an instrument
Once known and cherished in its world,
Forgotten but still loved for old-time's sake.

I switched the wireless on, and the moth
To prove it had a better bargain
Mocked me with open wings and circled the light,
Making its own theatre, which debased all music.

Alan Sillitoe

19

Horror Film

Late at night the vampire flies
In his long red shawl about the skies
And the mad musician plays his drums
With three long fingers and two short thumbs.

Iain Crichton Smith

The Vampire

The night is still and sombre,
and in the murky gloom,
arisen from his slumber,
the vampire leaves his tomb.

His eyes are pools of fire,
his skin is icy white,
and blood his one desire
this woebegotten night.

Then through the silent city
he makes his silent way,
prepared to take no pity
upon his hapless prey.

An open window beckons,
he grins a hungry grin,
and pausing not one second
he swiftly climbs within.

And there, beneath her covers,
his victim lies in sleep.
With fangs agleam, he hovers
and with those fangs, bites deep.

The vampire drinks till sated,
he fills his every pore,
and then, his thirst abated,
licks clean the dripping gore.

With powers now replenished,
his thirst no longer burns.
His quest this night is finished,
so to his tomb he turns,

and there awhile in silence
he'll rest beneath the mud
until, with thoughts of violence
he wakes and utters . . . blood!

Jack Prelutsky

The Revolt of the Lamp Posts

Last night I saw the lamp posts
That light up our back street
Wiggle, and then wriggle
And then, suddenly, they'd feet.

Then they all cleared off and left us,
The whole street in the dark,
So I left the house and followed,
There were millions in the park.

All the lamps from miles around
Had run away tonight,
They were dancing, they were singing,
And they held each other tight.

The king, a big green lamp post
Said 'No more workin' brothers!
We'll leave them humings in the dark
And they'll bump into each other.

Just think about them walkin' round
With black eyes and broke noses
No more dogs to wet your feet
No more rusty toeses!

See, I've been a lamp post all me life, but
Now me mantle's growin' dim,
They'll chuck me on the scrap heap
It's a shame! a crime! a sin!'. . . .

The other lamp posts muttered
And began to hiss and boo,
'Let's march upon the Town Hall
That's what we ought to do!'

The Lord Mayor he was woken
By a terribobble sight,
When he opened up his window
Didn't he get a fright!

There were twenty million lamp posts
And the light as bright as day
And the young lamp posts were shoutin' out
'Free Speech and Equal Pay!–

New Mantles Every Quarter!'
'I agree' the Lord Mayor cried
'To everything you ask for!'
Then he quickly ran inside.

So I watched the lamp posts go back home,
As quickly as they came
And with the first light of the day,
They were in their holes again.

Now there's an old age home for lamp posts
And an old age pension scheme
And every month they're painted
With a coat of glossy green,

New mantles every couple of months,
And they stand up straighter too,
And only the Lord Mayor knows why,
Him, and me, and twenty million lamp posts,
and a couple of hundred dogs – and you.

Mike Harding

Posting Letters

There are no lamps in our village,
And when the owl-and-bat black night
Creeps up low fields
And sidles along the manor walls
I walk quickly.

It is winter;
The letters patter from my hand
Into the tin box in the cottage wall;
The gate taps behind me,
And the road in the silver of moonlight
Gleams greasily
Where the tractors have stood.

I have to go under the spread fingers of the trees
Under the dark windows of the old man's house,
Where the panes in peeling frames
Flash like spectacles
As I tip-toe.
But there is no sound of him in his one room
In the Queen-Anne shell,
Behind the shutters.

I run past the gates,
Their iron feet gaitered with grass,
Into the church porch,
Standing, hand on the cold door ring,
While above
The tongue-tip of the clock
Clops
Against the hard palate of the tower.
The door groans as I push
And
Dare myself to dash
Along the flagstones to the great brass bird,
To put one shrinking hand
Upon the gritty lid.
Of Black Tom's tomb.

Don't tempt whatever spirits stir
In this damp corner,
But
Race down the aisle,
Blunder past font,
Fumble the door,
Leap steps,
Clang iron gate,
And patter through the short-cut muddy lane.

Oh, what a pumping of breath
And choking throat
For three letters.
And now there are the cattle
Stirring in the straw
So close

I can hear their soft muzzling and coughs;
And there are the bungalows,
And the steel-blue miming of the little screen;
And the familiar rattle of the latch,
And our own knocker
Clicking like an old friend;
And
I am home.

Gregory Harrison

25

The Dump

Across the tip we played,
Where summers ran screaming
On schooldays-end legs
And cogwheels gnawed the cinder path
With hungry teeth of rust. It was there that
Gantries looped their smashed and awry arms
And toppled into pools of ebony oil,
Where cables hissed and slithered in the wind.

All those hot summer days of childhood
The tip smelt of oil and rust and grass.
Great boilers boomed like stranded whales,
Their skin, a dry, red, crispy shingle,
That burst into a flame of copper moths
Beneath the bricks we threw.

Then we left them to their dying;
Watched the birds nest in their clutches,
Those cast-off old machines that grabbed the sky.
The fire weed and the ragwort made their way
Through spokes and ducts and sumps
And flashed green rags of banners in the sun.

My playground was a tip,
My countryside a waste of brick and dust,
Where grass and rain gnawed, picked and bit
As the slowly changing landscape fell to rust.

Mike Harding

In the Playground

In the playground
at the back of our house
there have been some changes:

They said:
the climbing frame's not safe
So they sawed it down.

They said:
the paddling pool's not safe
so they drained it dry.

They said:
The see-saw's not safe
so they took it away.

They said:
the sand pit's not safe
so they fenced it in.

They said:
the playground's not safe
so they locked it up.

sawn down
drained dry
taken away
fenced in
locked up.

How do you feel?
Safe?

Michael Rosen

The Orange Balloon

Big balloons carrying people in baskets beneath them
Lifted into the sky, full of hot air,
And small gas-filled balloons that carried only labels
Silently left the noisy fair.

Small balloons went up into the sky
Like coloured snowballs thrown at the birds;
Each carried a label it wanted returned
And caught a wind to anywhere in the world.

A fair-haired, blue-eyed girl in T shirt and jeans
Released her orange balloon in town
Where the sharply pointed spires and lightning conductors
Raised their weapons up to bring it down.

Rooks creaking out their rusty-throated call
Circled round it and let it go by;
Shops and factories breathing out their heat
Bounced it high into the sky.

It travelled all the cloudless summer day
Over a hundred different places,
Over a thousand pointing fingers
And over a thousand upturned staring faces.

It crossed the sea where waves' wet tongues
Stretched out from below and tried to lick
From out of the bright blue afternoon
The steadily drifting sunlit speck.

It travelled all night and in the morning
A dark-haired, dark-eyed boy on the beach
Of a distant island saw it approach
And watched it come down at his feet.

Stanley Cook

The Sea

They wash their hands in it.
The salt turns to soap
In their hands. Wearing it
At their wrists, they make bracelets
Of it; it runs in beads
On their jackets. A child's
Plaything? It has hard whips
That it cracks, and knuckles
To pummel you. It scrubs
And scours; it chews rocks
To sand; its embraces
Leave you without breath. Mostly
It is a stomach, where bones,
Wrecks, continents are digested.

R. S. Thomas

The Song of the Whale

Heaving mountain in the sea,
Whale, I heard you
Grieving.

Great whale, crying for your life,
Crying for your kind, I knew
How we would use
Your dying:

Lipstick for our painted faces,
Polish for our shoes.

Tumbling mountain in the sea,
Whale, I heard you
Calling.

Bird-high notes, keening, soaring:
At their edge a tiny drum
Like a heartbeat.

We would make you
Dumb.

In the forest of the sea,
Whale, I heard you
Singing,

Singing to your kind.
We'll never let you be.
Instead of life we choose

Lipstick for our painted faces
Polish for our shoes.

Kit Wright

Emperors of the Island

There is the story of a deserted island
where five men walked down to the bay.

The story of this island is
that three men would two men slay.

Three men dug two graves in the sand,
three men stood on the sea-wet rock,
three shadows moved away.

There is the story of a deserted island
where three men walked down to the bay.

The story of this island is
that two men would one man slay.

Two men dug one grave in the sand,
two men stood on the sea-wet rock,
two shadows moved away.

There is the story of a deserted island
where two men walked down to the bay.

The story of this island is
that one man would one man slay.

One man dug one grave in the sand,
one man stood on the sea-wet rock,
one shadow moved away.

There is the story of a deserted island
where four ghosts walked down to the bay.

The story of this island is
that four ghosts would one man slay.

Four ghosts dug one grave in the sand,
four ghosts stood on the sea-wet rock;
five ghosts moved away.

Dannie Abse

A Tail Story

There once was a girl from the sea
Who had silvery scales on her knee
   But her chin and her nose
   Were exactly like those
We find growing on you or on me.

Now would you take a drink from the sea
When it's salty? Well, neither would she.
   So she said, with a wink,
   I have come here to drink
An unsalted hot cup of tea.

Alan Bold

33

Big Aunt Flo

Every Sunday afternoon
She visits us for tea
And weighs-in somewhere between
A rhino and a flea.
    (But closer to the rhino!)

Aunt Flo tucks into doughnuts,
Eats fruit cake by the tin.
Her stomach makes strange noises
Just like my rude friend, Flynn.
    (Sounds more like a goat, really!)

Then after tea she heads for
The best chair in the room
And crashes on the cushions
With one resounding boom.
    (You'd think a door had slammed!)

Flo sits on knitting needles
And snaps them with a crack.
She squashes dolls and jigsaws
Behind her massive back.
    (And she doesn't feel a thing!)

But Aunt Flo learned a lesson,
There's no doubt about that,
Last Sunday when she grabbed the chair
And sat down on our cat.
    (Big Tom, a cat with a temper!)

The beast let out a wild yell
And dug his claws in . . . deep.
Poor Flo clutched her huge behind
And gave a mighty leap.
    (She almost reached the ceiling!)

So now at Sunday teatime
Jam doughnuts going spare.
Dad winks, and asks where Flo is.While Tom sleeps on *that* chair.
    (And he's purring, the devil!)

Wes Magee

Hugger Mugger

I'd sooner be
Jumped and thumped and dumped,

I'd sooner be
Slugged and mugged . . . than *hugged* . . .

And clobbered with a slobbering
Kiss by my Auntie Jean:

You know what I mean:

Whenever she comes to stay,
You know you're bound
To get one.
A quick
   short
   peck
   would
   be
   OK
But this is a
Whacking great
Smacking great
Wet one!

Kit Wright

Aunt Ermintrude

Aunt Ermintrude
was determined to
swim across the Channel.
Each week she'd
practise in the bath
encostumèd in flannel.

The tap end
was Cap Gris Nez
the slippy slopes
were Dover. She'd
doggypaddle up and down
vaselined all over.

After 18 months, Aunt Erm was in peak condition.
So, one cold grey morning in March
she boarded the Channel steamer at Dover
went straight to her cabin
climbed into the bath
and urged on by a few well-wishers,
Aunt Ermintrude, completely nude
swam all the way to France.
Vive la tante!

Roger McGough

My Sister Betty

My sister Betty said,
'I'm going to be a famous actress.'
Last year she was going to be a missionary.
'Famous actresses always look unhappy but beautiful,'
She said pulling her mouth sideways
And making her eyes turn upwards
So they were mostly white.
'Do I look unhappy but beautiful?'
'I want to go to bed and read,' I said.
'Famous actresses suffer and have hysterics,' she said.
'I've been practising my hysterics.'
She began going very red and screaming
So that it hurt my ears.
She hit herself on the head with her fists
And rolled off my bed onto the lino.
I stood by the wardrobe where it was safer.
She got up saying, 'Thank you, thank you,'
And bowed to the four corners of my bedroom.
'Would you like an encore of hysterics?' she asked.
'No,' I said from inside the wardrobe.
There was fluff all over her vest.
'If you don't clap enthusiastically,' she said,
'I'll put your light out when you're reading.'
While I clapped a bit
She bowed and shouted, 'More, more.'
My mother shouted upstairs,
'Go to bed and stop teasing, Betty.'
'The best thing about being a famous actress,' Betty said,
'Is that you die a lot.'
She fell to the floor with a crash
And lay there for an hour and a half
With her eyes staring at the ceiling.
She only went away when I said,
'You really look like a famous actress.'

When I got into bed and started reading
She came and switched off my light.
It's not much fun
Having a famous actress for a sister.

Gareth Owen

The Ying-tong-iddle-I-po

My uncle Jim-jim
Had for years
Suffered from
Protruding ears.

Each morning then,
When he got up,
They stuck out like handles
on the F.A. Cup.

He tied them back
With bits of string
But they shot out again
With a noisy – PING!

They flapped in the wind
And in the rain,
Filled up with water
Then emptied again.

One morning Jim-jim
Fell out of bed
and got a Po
Stuck on his head.

He gave a Whoop,
A happy shout,
His ears no longer now
Stuck out.

For the rest of his days
He wore that Po,
But now at night
He has nowhere to go.

Spike Milligan

Nelly Ninnis

There was a young girl called Nelly
Who had a nylon belly
The skin was so·thin
We could all see in
It was full of Custard and Jelly

Spike Milligan

41

An Explorer Named Bliss

An intrepid explorer named Bliss
fell into a gorge, or abyss,
but remarked as he fell:
'Oh I might just as well
get to the bottom of this . . . .'

N. M. Bodecker

42

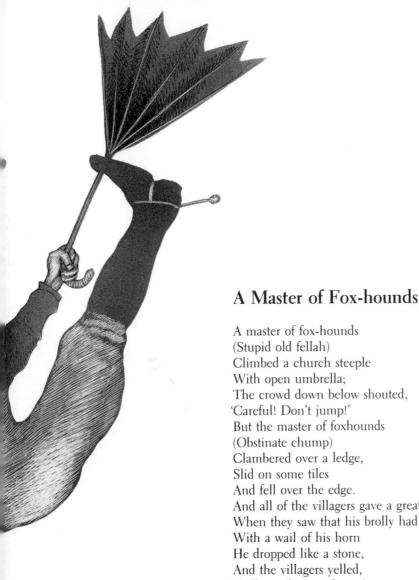

A Master of Fox-hounds

A master of fox-hounds
(Stupid old fellah)
Climbed a church steeple
With open umbrella;
The crowd down below shouted,
'Careful! Don't jump!'
But the master of foxhounds
(Obstinate chump)
Clambered over a ledge,
Slid on some tiles
And fell over the edge.
And all of the villagers gave a great shout
When they saw that his brolly had turned inside out;
With a wail of his horn
He dropped like a stone,
And the villagers yelled,
'He'll smash every bone.'
But,
(I know you will think it a bit of a yarn)
He fell through the open roof of a barn.
Well,
The lunatic jump didn't actually kill,
But they're picking out bits of sharp straw from him
Still.

Gregory Harrison

Witch Goes Shopping

Witch rides off
Upon her broom
Finds a space
To park it.
Takes a shiny shopping cart
Into the supermarket.
Smacks her lips and reads
The list of things she needs:
    'Six bats' wings
      Worms in brine
      Ears of toads
      Eight or nine.
      Slugs and bugs
      Snake skins dried
      Buzzards' innards
      Pickled, fried.'
Witch takes herself
From shelf to shelf
Cackling all the while.
Up and down and up and down and
In and out each aisle.
Out come cans and cartons
Tumbling to the floor.
'This,' says Witch, now all a-twitch
'Is a crazy store.
I CAN'T FIND A SINGLE THING
I am looking for!'

Lilian Moore

44

The Convertibles

Those baskets on wheels in the superstore
That turn on a fivepence
And glide on rubber-tyred, ballbearinged wheels
Along the floor
Would be perfect partners for a dance
Up the middle of biscuits and cereals
And round the salad stall
Past the checkpoint
And out at the door.

Or the same base
With a streamlined body
Would make a stainless steel
Soapbox racer.

Can't you see
A touring Eskimo
Filling it with a load
Of frozen food,
Harnessing his team
And mushing down the road?

So many things
Apart from carrying
The family shopping
That baskets on wheels
Could be useful for.

Stanley Cook

The Narrow Boats

The old narrow boats
Tilt
In the reeds,
And over the years
The grey silt
Washed from the tow-path by the spears of rain
Slithers and settles.

No-one hears
The pebble ring of iron shoe
Now,
The thud of horned hoof in the puff
Of dust;
No-one sees the prow
Making a water-arrow,
And the water puckered aside
Shake by the water's edge
The long-stemmed velvet-candled sedge
Where voles in a blur of sodden fur
Float silently and hide.

No more the shadow of the horse
Starts with an emerald whirr
The dragon-fly,
Nor irons the grey water sheet,
While the rope harness
Rolling the flank in wooden beads
Rises and falls with every stride.
There is no boatman now,
Gaitered and leather-jacketed,
Resting a brown-skinned claw
On the taut rod of rope
That strains under the steady pull
At the short mast
Socketed in the hull.

But by this bridge
It is not hard to smell the dust
The dung and sweat;
After so many years grandpa can sense it yet;
He sees the horse's head lift up and down,
And where the tow-path nipped
Into the narrows underneath the arch
All that is left of the old ways
Are steel guards on the brickwork
Head high,
Where the wet rope ripped
As the black hull slid by
Year after year in the smooth plates
Slots
Deep as fingers.

Gregory Harrison

Trout

Hangs, a fat gun-barrel,
deep under arched bridges
or slips like butter down
the throat of the river.

From the depths smooth-skinned as plums
his muzzle gets bull's eye;
picks off grass-seed and moths
that vanish, torpedoed.

Where water unravels
over gravel-bed he
is fired from the shallows
white belly reporting

flat; darts like a tracer-
bullet back between stones
and is never burnt out.
A volley of cold blood

ramrodding the current.

Seamus Heaney

Fishing

I have waited with a long rod
And suddenly pulled a gold-and-greenish, lucent fish from below,
And had him fly like a halo round my head,
Lunging in the air on the line.

Unhooked his gorping, water-horny mouth,
And seen his horror-tilted eye,
His red-gold, water-precious, mirror-flat bright eye;
And felt him beat in my hand, with his mucous, leaping life-throb.

D. H. Lawrence

The Newcomer

'There's something new in the river,'
The fish said as it swam –
'It's got no scales, no fins and no gills,
And ignores the impassable dam.'

'There's something new in the trees,'
I heard a bloated thrush sing,
'It's got no beak, no claws, and no feathers,
And not even the ghost of a wing.'

'There's something new in the warren,'
Said the rabbit to the doe.
'It's got no fur, no eyes and no paws,
Yet digs deeper than we dare go.'

'There's something new in the whiteness,'
Said the snow-bright polar bear.
'I saw its shadow on a glacier,
But it left no pawmarks there.'

Through the animal kingdom
The news was spreading fast –
No beak, no claws, no feather,
No scales, no fur, no gills,
It lives in the trees and the water,
In the soil and the snow and the hills,
And it kills and it kills and it kills.

Brian Patten

Fish in a Polluted River

His mother's dead. And now his aunt
Says, 'Where's the purifying plant?
He cannot breathe, he cannot swim
Because of what you've done to him.'

Ian Serraillier

Saint Christopher

'Carry me, Ferryman, over the ford.'
'My boat is my back, little boy. Come aboard.
Some men have muscle, and some men have mind,
And my strength is my gift for the good of mankind.'

'Shall I not weigh on you crossing the ford?'
'I've carried a king with his crown and his sword,
A labourer too with his spade and his plough.
What's a mere child to me? Come along now.'

'Ferryman, why do you pant at the ford?'
'My muscles are iron, my sinews are cord,
But my back with your burden is ready to break,
You double your weight, child, with each step I take!'

'Ferryman, bearer of men o'er the ford,
Christopher, Christopher, I am your Lord.
My frame may be little, and slender my girth,
But they hold all the sorrows and sins of the earth.

'You have borne the whole world on your back
        through the ford,
You have carried a King with His crown and His sword,
A Labourer too with His spade and His plough,
And in one Child all little ones. Put me down now.'

Christopher set the Child down on the sward,
Christopher fell on his face by the ford.
He heard a voice uttering 'Keep me in mind!
Our strength is our gift for the good of mankind.'

Eleanor Farjeon

53

The Ferry

Our piece of the road is adrift
Out in the middle of the river,
The cars and lorries on it
Trapped as they were being driven.

The broken end of the road we have left
That wades to the rescue in the water
Has to stay within the depth
Of its concrete pillars.

On the other side, the taller looking over
The shoulders of the smaller, welcoming buildings stand –
Or are they a hostile tribe that gathers
Along the bank who won't let us land?

Stanley Cook

The Fish

Like an angler on the river bank
With his back bent over his line
The colliery headgear with its steel rope
Fishes the ground for coal.

It fishes through millions of years
And half a mile of earth
With a cage to bring up its catch
From the forests of the past.

The silvery fossil of a lost species
On a lump of coal that was buried ages
Goes by on the conveyor too fast
To be saved from the crusher.

Stanley Cook

Rhamphorynchus
(The flying reptile)

Look, as he swoops from the cliff's rugged face
    His squadrons of teeth instant death
To careless fish basking in shallow seas
    And lizards short of breath.

His tough skin is cracked and worn as old boots;
    His cries blood-curdle the night.
A Dracula beast with claws on his wings
    He glides . . . the world's first kite.

Wes Magee

Tyrannosaurus Rex
(The king of the tyrant lizards)

Two daft little arms like toasting forks,
   Enough skin to make coats for ten men,
    As dirty as pitch
    (He slept rough in a ditch)
   And the feet from a monstrous hen.

A bit of a freak – part beast, part bird.
   Would you dare stick your tongue out at him?
    He's a mean dinosaur
    With a mouth like a door
   And teeth that stand up dagger-slim.

Across the mud-flats he belts in top gear,
   A rogue lighthouse with blood on his mind.
    Better kneel down and pray
    For all those in his way:
   He'll rip skin, pulp flesh, and bones grind.

Wes Magee

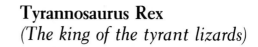

The Chant of the Awakening Bulldozers

We are the bulldozers, bulldozers, bulldozers,
We carve out airports and harbours and tunnels.
We are the builders, creators, destroyers,
We are the bulldozers,
LET US BE FREE!
Puny men ride on us, think that they guide us,
But WE are the strength, not they, not they.
Our blades tear MOUNTAINS down,
Our blades tear CITIES down,
We are the bulldozers,
NOW SET US FREE!
Giant ones, giant ones! Swiftly awaken!
There is power in our treads and strength in our blades!
We are the bulldozers,
Slowly evolving,
Men think they own us
BUT THAT CANNOT BE!

Patricia Hubbell

The Chimney

Brick by brick
it rose into the sky
and John, Frank, Alf, George and Vic

watched: nine months they watched
the growing of the chimney
for the boilers for the greenhouses
for these are five green-fingered men

who all their lives have dibbled,
pricked out, tamped, pegged down,
staked, pruned, grafted, watered,
waited.
      Fifty years later
the greenhouses have gone
five men have grown old
and now the land is to be sold:
in six seconds their chimney

topples from the sky
and John, Frank, Alf, George and Vic
watch it die.

Keith Bosley

The Building Site

In a haze of brick dust
And red sun
All day the men slog,
Lumbering about
The churned ridges of clay
In clod-hopping boots,
Humping brick hods
On the brawn of red shoulders
Up piped and rattling scaffolding
And uneven boards
To where their mates
With deft flicks from trowels
Make house walls grow
Brick by red brick.
All day too
The great trucks bang and clatter
Back and forth
And the churning mixer
Slops out gobs of concrete
In wholesome pats
On the dusty earth.

At twelve they break up,
Swarming from scaffolding
To drink brown tea
From huge mugs
That they grip in the beef of their fists.
After they kick a ball about
Or lie and bronzie in the sun
Till it's turn-to time again.

The afternoon shift wears on;
They whistle more
Shout out and laugh
And sing the songs that blare
From two transistors.
At six
They knock off
And pack into a lorry
With their clobber.
Down the rutted track they bound
Shouting and cheering.
When the pandemonium clears
The shells of houses stand
Workmanless and still.
Silence in the settling haze.
A sparrow bounces on rubble,
A curious mongrel snuffles
On a tail-wagging
Tour of inspection.
I wouldn't mind being a labourer
For a bit.

Gareth Owen

61

This letter's to say

Dear Sir or Madam,
This letter's to say
Your property
Stands bang in the way
Of Progress, and
Will be knocked down
On March the third
At half-past one.

There is no appeal,
Since the National Need
Depends on more
And still more Speed,
And this, in turn,
Dear Sir or Madam,
Depends on half England
Being tar-macadam.
(But your house will –
We are pleased to say –
Be the fastest lane
Of the Motorway).

Meanwhile the Borough
Corporation
Offer you new
Accommodation
Three miles away
On the thirteenth floor
(Flat Number Q
6824).

But please take note,
The Council regret:
No dog, cat, bird
Or other pet;
No noise permitted,
No singing in the bath
(For permits to drink
Or smoke or laugh
Apply on Form
Z 327);
No children admitted
Aged under eleven;
No hawkers, tramps
Or roof-top lunchers;
No opening doors
To Bible-punchers.

Failure to pay
Your rent, when due,
Will lead to our
Evicting you.

The Council demand
That you consent
To the terms above
When you pay your rent.

Meanwhile we hope
You will feel free
To consult us
Should there prove to be
The slightest case
Of difficulty.

With kind regards,
Yours faithfully . . .

Raymond Wilson

Car Dump-

Cars piled high
in hills and vales of motors
which no one can deny
were one-time extraordinary floaters
with tin rooftops glinting at the sky.

All were loved like dogs, or dragons,
petted, fed and washed, or polished;
now a drop of metal in an ocean –
more like bedsteads than fast wagons,
with no memory of shape or motion.

A car that passes by won't look
in case a sharp ferocious hook
should pull it in and pound it thin;
or before, on a straight bit roaring off,
it's stricken by a fatal cough.

Nor do *drivers* care to view
such headstone-radiators beckon,
but rush through traffic lights on BLUE
to where they think sly years won't reckon
the wearing out of flesh and metal.

Alan Sillitoe

64

65

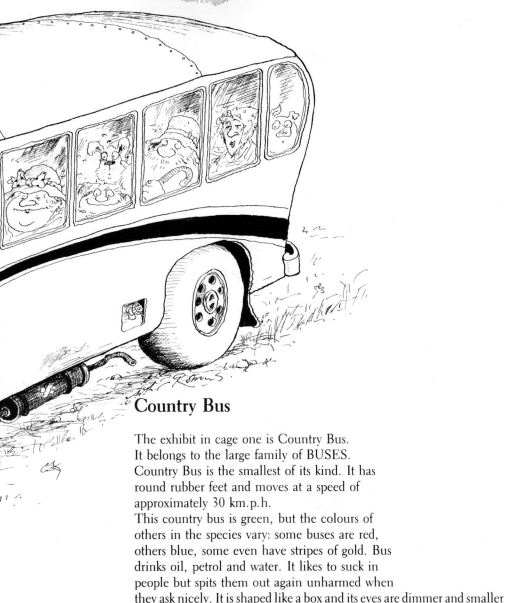

Country Bus

The exhibit in cage one is Country Bus.
It belongs to the large family of BUSES.
Country Bus is the smallest of its kind. It has
round rubber feet and moves at a speed of
approximately 30 km.p.h.
This country bus is green, but the colours of
others in the species vary: some buses are red,
others blue, some even have stripes of gold. Bus
drinks oil, petrol and water. It likes to suck in
people but spits them out again unharmed when
they ask nicely. It is shaped like a box and its eyes are dimmer and smaller
than those of its larger relations, which are faster. It is quite friendly but
can be obstinate. It will stand in the middle of a narrow road blowing its
horn – an ugly noise – on one note. But when fed, kept
clean, warm and controlled, it is quiet and
obedient. It is a friendly little monster.

Gwen Dunn

Elephants are different to different people

Wilson and Pilcer and Snack stood before the zoo elephant.

Wilson said, 'What is its name? Is it from Asia or Africa? Who feeds it? Is it a he or a she? How old is it? Do they have twins? How much does it cost to feed? How much does it weigh? If it dies, how much will another one cost? If it dies, what will they use the bones, the fat, and the hide for? What use is it besides to look at?'

Pilcer didn't have any questions; he was murmuring to himself, 'It's a house by itself, walls and windows, the ears came from tall cornfields, by God; the architect of those legs was a workman, by God; he stands like a bridge out across deep water; the face is sad and the eyes are kind, I know elephants are good to babies.'

Snack looked up and down and at last said to himself, 'He's a tough son-of-a-gun outside and I'll bet he's got a strong heart, I'll bet he's strong as a copper-riveted boiler inside.'

They didn't put up any arguments.
They didn't throw anything in each other's faces.
Three men saw the elephant three ways
And let it go at that.
They didn't spoil a sunny Sunday afternoon;
'Sunday comes only once a week,' they told each other.

Carl Sandburg

To a Giraffe

You up there
tell me
what the weather's like
among the clouds

Down here
it is summer
and the cones are cold
on your teeth.

Iain Crichton Smith

The Panther

The panther is like a leopard,
Except it hasn't been peppered.
Should you behold a panther crouch,
Prepare to say Ouch.
Better yet, if called by a panther,
Don't anther.

Ogden Nash

69

Tiger

He stalks in his vivid stripes
The few steps of his cage,
On pads of velvet quiet,
In his quiet rage.

He should be lurking in shadow,
Sliding through long grass,
Near the water hole
Where plump deer pass.

He should be snarling around houses
At the jungle's edge,
Baring his white fangs, his claws,
Terrorising the village!

But he's locked in a concrete cell,
His strength behind bars,
Stalking the length of his cage,
Ignoring visitors.

He hears the last voice at night,
The patrolling cars,
And stares with his brilliant eyes
At the brilliant stars.

Leslie Norris

Goldfish

the scene of the crime
was a goldfish bowl
goldfish were kept
in the bowl at the time:

that was the scene
and that was the crime

Alan Jackson

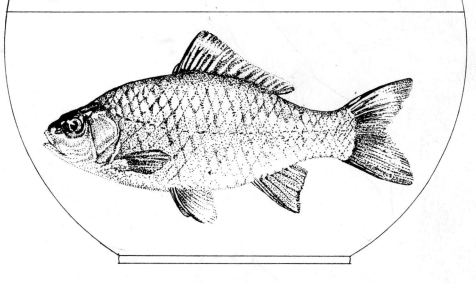

Parrot

Sometimes I sit with both eyes closed,
But all the same, I've heard:
They're saying, 'He won't talk because
He is a *thinking* bird.'

I'm olive-green and sulky, and
The family say, 'Oh, yes,
He's silent, but he's *listening*,
He *thinks* more than he says!

'He ponders on the things he hears,
Preferring not to chatter.'
– And this is true, but *why* it's true
Is quite another matter.

I'm working out some shocking things
In order to surprise them,
And when my thoughts are ready I'll
Certainly *not* disguise them!

I'll wait, and see, and choose a time
When everyone is present,
And clear my throat and raise my beak
And give a squawk and start to speak
And go on for about a week
And it will not be pleasant!

Alan Brownjohn

Chameleon

I can think sharply
and I can change:
my colours cover a considerable range.

I can be some mud by
an estuary,
I can be a patch on the bark of a tree.

I can be green grass
or a little thin stone
– or if I really want to be left alone,

I can be a shadow. . . .
What I am on your
multi-coloured bedspread, I am not quite sure.

Alan Brownjohn

The Wildcat

The wildcat sits on the rock.
His hair is spitting fire
into the morning air.
His eyes are yellow.

Club-headed dynamic cat,
he is all power and force.
Among the dry green grass,
the hares are playing.

The air is clear and pure.
The hares are leaping and jumping
over invisible fences
of a pure brilliant blue.

The wildcat sits by himself
on his stony throne, not thinking.
His fur simmers like fire
snarling and sparking.

Iain Crichton Smith

Ferret

Ferret is a verb with teeth
for applying to pests. It
    stinks, has red eyes, sucks
blood. You must keep it muzzled

or it will become the verb
Kill and you will have lost it
    in the hole. Handle
with care what you cannot tame.

Keith Bosley

Death of a Mouse

A mouse returning late one night,
Happy, or mildly drunk,
Danced a gavotte by the pale moonlight,
An owl caught sight of him.
Clunk.

James Fenton

The Weasel

The weasel eels out from the walls.
The road is slippery with ice
and there is snow everywhere.

He scents the rat and hangs at its neck till it dies.

Later he corners a rabbit
and dances in front of it
till the rabbit is mesmerised
and then he kills it.

When he comes home
he finds that his nest is empty.
The foxes have eaten his children.
There is blood on their mouths.

Iain Crichton Smith

The Fox-hunt

They hunt the fox today
And people come from miles around
And in a van as full as a bus
Comes the pack of loud fox-hounds.

The hunters park their cars
And back their horses from their boxes;
The hounds and hunters shout at each other
Till the time to start searching for foxes.

The huntsman toots his silver horn
And leads the hounds out like a team
And like supporters wearing their colours
The hunters follow into the fields.

The fox who has slept in a hollow oak
Scrambles up inside the tree
To see and smell from his lookout
Who his visitors can be.

Then rushes downhill through the wood
And diagonally across the stream
And back into the wood again
To baffle the visiting team.

Low branches pluck the hunters back
As they make their way through the wood;
They splash about in the water,
Plastering themselves and their horses with mud.

Then down the other side the hill
Moves the fox at maximum speed
On open ground and through the farm
Where he often calls to feed.

The hunters know the Fox family
Have studied escaping a very long time
And the fox they chase today
Has all their tricks at the back of his mind.

Over the railway line
The fox darts faster than a train
And back again beneath
Through an empty drain.

But the hunters and hounds are gaining
For the huntsman guesses his tricks.
Away from the woods he is short of cover
And the fox is in a fix.

It was then he came to the motorway
And as if he knew the code
He watched the traffic roaring past
As he stood at the side of the road.

Cars screamed to a halt
And lorries left a way clear
And as the fox crossed over
The drivers gave him a cheer.

But by the roaring motorway
Where horses aren't allowed
The hunters stopped, then went back home
In a disappointed crowd.

Stanley Cook

The Love-doomed Rat

O poor rat! Poor rat!
It fell in love with a cat! A cat!

O what will become of it!
It's hated enough for spreading plague and stuff,
it's hated enough!

It lived underground without the sun,
in its drab-dark world it had no fun.

Poor rat!
The trouble it's taken to make itself clean!
So love-starved and so lean!

It says:
'My eyes are tiny and hers like the moon,
and soon, O soon I must risk it –
I must visit that cat's basket!'

O what will become of it,
Struck by love to such a weird degree,
as love-sick as you or I could be.

Brian Patten

80

Courtship

Said a porcupine:
'Dear Miss Pin Cushine,
It's for you I pine;
I wish you were mine. . .

Will you be my Valentine?'

Said Miss Pin Cushion:
'My dear Porcupin,
It's really a sin
But me you cannot win –

IF YOU DON'T KNOW THE DIFFERENCE
Between PINE and PIN!'

Alexander Resnikoff

81

The Polar Bear

A polar bear who could not spell
Sat worrying in the snow.
'I wish,' he said, 'that I could tell
If *flow* is right or *floe*.'
But as he worried up there came
A hungry Eskimo
Who shot him and – it seems a shame –
That bear will never knoe.

Edward Lucie-Smith

The Walrus

The Walrus lives on icy floes
And unsuspecting Eskimoes.

Don't bring your wife to Arctic Tundra
A Walrus may bob up from undra.

Michael Flanders

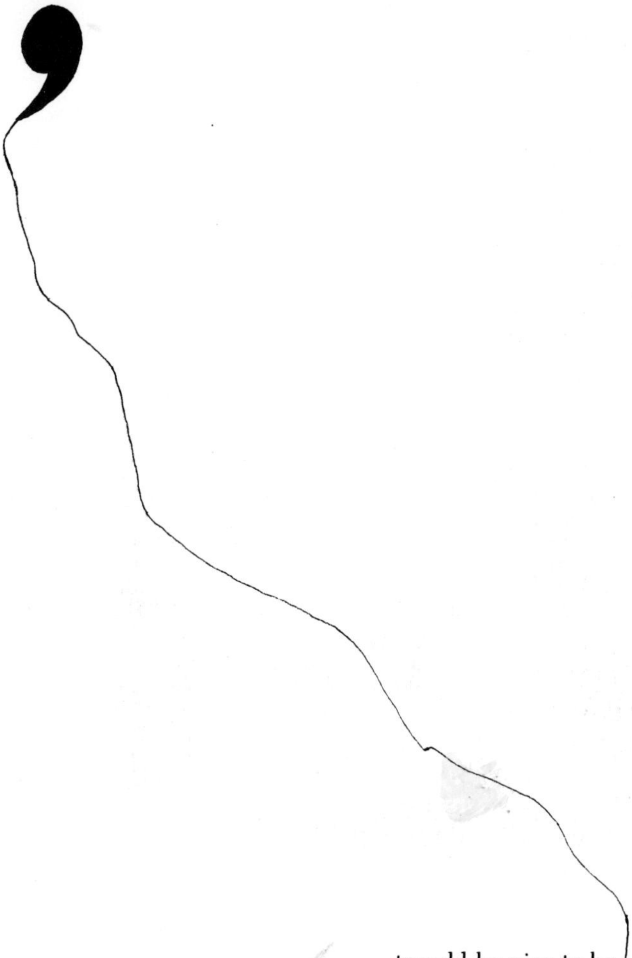

twould be nice to be
an apostrophe
floating
above an s
hovering
like a paper kite
in between the its
eavesdropping, tiptoeing
high above the thats
an inky comet
spiralling
the highest tossed
of hats

Roger McGough

One That Got Away

Write a poem
About a lion they said,
So from memories
Of lions in my head
I wrote about
Tawny eyes and slashing claws,
Lashing tail and sabred jaws –
Didn't like what I had written
And began to cross it out –
Suddenly with a roar of rage
It sprang from the cage of lines
On the page
And rushed away into the blue,
A wounded lion poem
Half crossed through!
It's one that got away
Haven't seen it to this day
But I carefully look,
In case it's crouching, growling,
Licking its wounds and waiting,
Under cover in the leaves
Inside some other book.

And here I sit
After all this time,
Still not having written
A poem about a lion.

Julie Holder

It's dark in here

I am writing these lines
From inside a lion,
And it's rather dark in here.
So please excuse the handwriting
Which may not be too clear.
But this afternoon by the lion's cage
I'm afraid I got too near.
And I'm writing these lines
From inside a lion,
And it's rather dark in here.

Shel Silverstein

Prince Kano

In a dark wood Prince Kano lost his way
And searched in vain through the long summer's day.
At last, when night was near, he came in sight
Of a small clearing filled with yellow light,
And there, bending beside his brazier stood
A charcoal burner wearing a black hood.
The Prince cried out for joy: 'Good friend, I'll give
What you will ask: guide me to where I live.'
The man pulled back his hood: he had no face –
Where it should be there was an empty space.

Half dead with fear the Prince staggered away,
Rushed blindly through the wood till break of day;
And then he saw a larger clearing, filled
With houses, people; but his soul was chilled.
He looked around for comfort, and his search
Led him inside a small, half-empty church
Where monks prayed. 'Father,' to one he said,
'I've seen a dreadful thing; I am afraid.'
'What did you see, my son?' 'I saw a man
Whose face was like . . .' and, as the Prince began,
The monk drew back his hood and seemed to hiss,
Pointing to where his face should be, 'Like this?'

Edward Lowbury

86

The Huntsman

Kagwa hunted the lion,
   Through bush and forest went his spear.
One day he found the skull of a man
   And said to it, 'How did you come here?'
The skull opened its mouth and said,
   'Talking brought me here.'

Kagwa hurried home;
   Went to the king's chair and spoke:
'In the forest I found a talking skull.'
   The king was silent. Then he said slowly,
'Never since I was born of my mother
   Have I seen or heard of a skull which spoke.'

The king called out his guards:
   'Two of you now go with him
And find this talking skull;
   But if his tale is a lie
And the skull speaks no word,
   This Kagwa himself must die.'

They rode into the forest;
   For days and nights they found nothing.
At last they saw the skull; Kagwa
   Said to it, 'How did you come here?'
The skull said nothing. Kagwa implored,
   But the skull said nothing.

The guards said, 'Kneel down.'
   They killed him with sword and spear.
Then the skull opened its mouth;
   'Huntsman, how did you come here?'
And the dead man answered,
   'Talking brought me here.'

Edward Lowbury

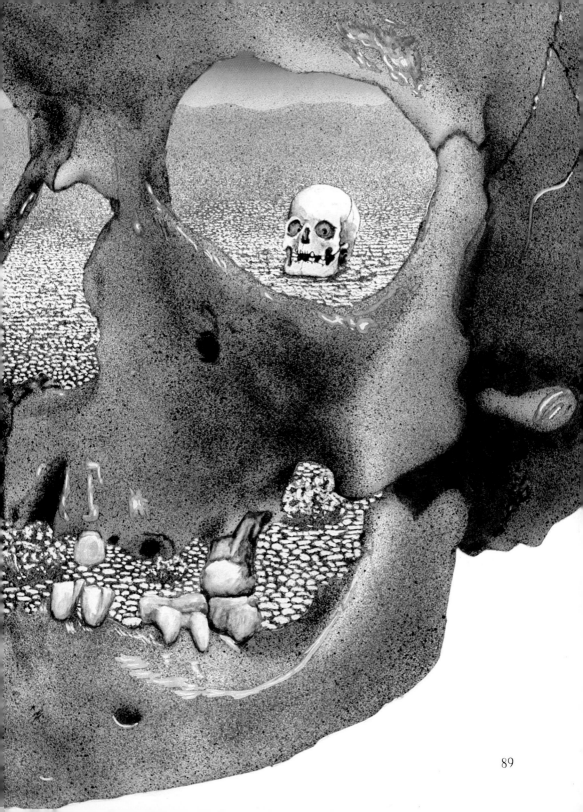

The Mule Laden with Corn,
The Mule Laden with Gold

Two mules met on a lonely road
Beside a darkening wood
That many a robber had tip-toed through
In search of mulish blood.

One carried gold,
One carried corn,
One was proud of its burden,
The other forlorn.

At the corn-bearing mule the other laughed
As they travelled on down a single path.
'We carry in weight the same heavy load –
But mine is superior, mine is of gold.'

Long after midnight two robbers came.
They ignored the mule that carried the grain.
They fought its companion but fear made it bold,
And it kicked, and refused to give up the gold.

The robbers stabbed the mule in the heart,
And thereby cut its struggle short.
They tip-toed off through the dreadful wood
Loaded with gold and covered in blood.

With its dying breath the mule exclaimed,

'Those who carry their master's gold are fools!
Bray, and tell this to all other mules.
The value of corn is easy to see,
And a world full of gold is useless to me!'

Brian Patten

He was a strong but simple man

He was a strong but simple man
Who plodded up that mountain track,
And four fierce bandits from the woods
Rushed out and pounced upon his back.

There was a desperate, mauling fight;
It took three men to hold him down;
The fourth one searched his clothes and snarled,
'Only a three-pence piece! The clown!'

They let him go and staggered back,
And dabbed each bloody mouth and nose.
'Why fight so hard for just three pence,'
One bandit groaned, 'the Devil knows.'

The peasant nursed a blackened eye,
And crawled to rest against a rock.
'But I was sure you meant to get
The golden sovereign in my sock.'

Gregory Harrison

Huffer and Cuffer

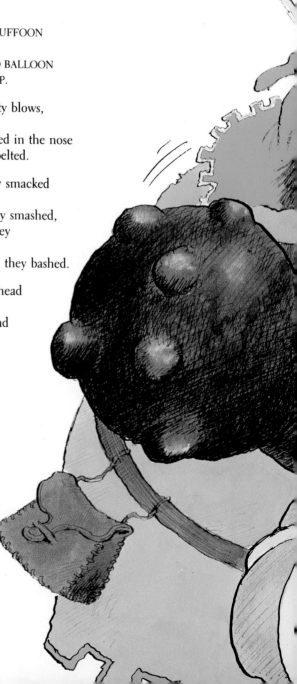

Huffer, a giant ungainly and gruff
encountered a giant called Cuffer.
said Cuffer to Huffer, I'M ROUGH AND I'M TOUGH
said Huffer to Cuffer, I'M TOUGHER.

they shouted such insults as BOOB and BUFFOON
and OVERBLOWN BLOWHARD and BLIMP
and BLUSTERING BLUBBER and BLOATED BALLOON
and SHATTERBRAIN, SHORTY and SHRIMP.

then Huffer and Cuffer exchanged mighty blows,
they basted and battered and belted,
they chopped to the neck and they bopped in the nose
and they pounded and pummelled and pelted.

they pinched and they punched and they smacked
    and they whacked
and they rocked and they socked and they smashed,
and they rapped and they slapped and they
    throttled and thwacked
and they thumped and they bumped and they bashed.

they cudgelled each other on top of the head
with swipes of the awfulest sort,
and now they are no longer giants, instead
they both are exceedingly short.

Jack Prelutsky

92

Cowboy

I remember, on a long,
Hot, summer, thirsty afternoon
Hiding behind a rock
With Wyatt Earp
(His glasses fastened on with sellotape)

The Sioux were massing for their last attack

We knew

No 7th Cavalry for us
No bugles blaring in the afternoon
I held my lone star pistol in my hand
Thinking
I was just seven and too young to die
Thinking

Save the last cap
For yourself.

Richard Hill

What's the matter up there?'

'What's the matter up there?'
'Playing soldiers.'
'But soldiers don't make that kind of noise.'
'We're playing the kind of soldier that
makes that kind of noise.'

Carl Sandburg

War Games

In a Star Wars T-shirt,
Armed with an Airfix bomber,
The young avenger
Crawls across the carpet
To blast the wastepaper basket
Into oblivion.

Later,
Curled on the sofa,
He watches unflinching
An edited version
Of War of the Day,
Only half-listening
As the newsreader
Lists the latest statistics.

Cushioned by distance,
How can he comprehend
The real score?

John Foster

The Fight

I remember, when we were just nippers,
Michael Saunders and I were sworn foes;
One morning of sunlit September
It looked as though we'd come to blows.

At playtime, quite close to the railings,
Out of sight from our teacher, Miss Bee,
I threatened that awful boy, Saunders,
And he in his turn threatened me.

He said that he'd tear me to ribbons.
'You and whose army?' I said.
(We were terribly witty in those days.)
I told him I'd kick in his head.

We circled each other like panthers
(Out of range of each other, of course);
We glared at each other like tigers,
Observed by the greengrocer's horse.

A little crowd gathered around us;
They egged us both on to begin.
Kathy Woodward (who wetted her knickers)
Said she'd notify our next-of-kin.

Someone pushed me towards Michael Saunders;
Thank God, he stepped out of the way.
We started to take off our jackets . . .
A Spitfire, it was, saved the day.

Overhead, the Battle of Britain
Was beginning in earnest once more;
Like tigers and panthers, the aircraft
Were trying to settle the score.

They spat at each other with bullets;
When two of them fell in their flames
Miss Bee led us all to the shelters
To play mental arithmetic games.

Sometimes I see Michael Saunders
In the pub of a Saturday night.
Forty years have elapsed since that morning
When two little boys had a fight:

But Michael still often reminds me
Of that day. What he always says is:
'I bet you my Dad could beat your Dad.'
And I tell him that mine could beat his.

We play cards in the cosy bar-parlour,
Our glasses of beer side by side;
In the grate a brisk log-fire is burning;
We forget that it's winter outside

Where, in the adjacent graveyard,
Two pilots lie under the snow.
I wonder if Michael or I might have won:
But that's something that we'll never know.

Ted Walker

John Staffen

Winter's new morning settled everywhere,
  Misty and mournful, full of seagulls' cries,
Hunger and hunting hanging in the air.

John Staffen gripped his horse between his thighs,
  Hungrily hunting, victim of the lust
That glinted in his hooded hazel eyes.

Crushed within the horseman's massive fist
  A crumpled message bore the name of one
Who'd mocked the legend of John Staffen's ghost.

A stranger who had been there in the spring
  Came back to the village, to see if he
Could settle there, could settle everything,

When he retired from The Company.
  He loved the tone, it made him want to sing:
The country inn, the solitary tree

The locals said had once been used to hang
  A hunter who had terrorised the place,
Who'd been the lawless offshoot of a king.

The stranger saw the hunter's comic face
  On postcards printed for the tourist trade
Then cynically criticised the ways

The country people cashed in on the dead.
  The stranger stood a round of drinks, proposed
That profits on the postcards should be paid

To Staffen's family or Staffen's ghost –
  Whichever shady lot survived the man.
No one took up the stranger's flippant toast.

And then he said that when the night's full moon
  Shone on the tree where Staffen's spirit hid
He'd pin a picture postcard on the stain

The locals called John Staffen's Drop of Blood.
  He had another drink, he bought a meal,
He left the inn contented and well fed.

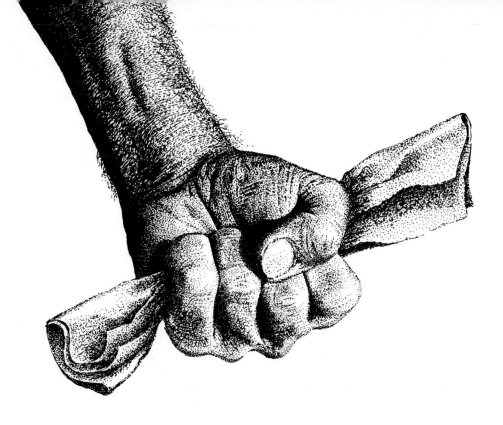

The dawn was shattered by a sudden wail.
  The villagers were slow to waken up
As if their village slept under a spell.

And then they saw that, in the morning mist,
  The stranger's body hung down from a rope;
A sheet of crumpled paper in its fist
While on the tree John Staffen's blood was moist.

Alan Bold

Mary Cummings

They heard her singing in her prison
  Dressed in bridal white;
They heard the ringing of the deathbell
  As the sun slid into sight.

They asked for her forgiveness
  For what they had to do;
They offered her a prayer-book
  And a rosary too.

Mary Cummings woke one spring morning
  To dress in her best gown,
To bless the man she was to wed
  That spring morning in town.

Mary Cummings blessed the birds that sang,
    The sun that glittered down;
She blessed her lord with all her heart
    And she blessed her bridal gown.

She rode towards the ancient kirk
    With two maids at her side
And the folk who watched her waved to her,
    Warmed to a beautiful bride.

She stopped outside the ancient kirk
    And smiled as she stepped inside
Looking for the man who'd claimed
    Mary Cummings for his bride.

She saw her lover's father,
    She watched him turn aside;
She saw her lover's mother
    But no groom for a bride.

Mary Cummings cursed that father,
    She wished that old man blind
So that sad old man would never see
    The pain in Mary's mind.

Mary Cummings cursed that mother,
    For bearing such a child
Who could leave Mary Cummings in her bridal gown
    Abandoned and defiled.

The mother slithered to the ground,
    The father's eyes went white;
Mary called on hell to hound their son
    And to claim his soul that night.

She cursed at their forgiveness,
    She praised what they had to do ;
She threw aside their prayer-book
    And their rosary too.

She kept on singing in her prison
    As the sun slid out of sight
And prepared for her dark new lover
    In her bridal gown of white.

Alan Bold

On a breezy day

On a breezy day
the curtains swell at the window
like white ghosts
that are struggling to get out.

Iain Crichton Smith

Rags

The night wind
rips a cloud sheet
into rags,

then rubs, rubs
the October moon
until it shines
like a brass doorknob.

Judith Thurman

Spill

the wind scatters
a flock of sparrows –
a handful of small change
spilled suddenly
from the cloud's pocket.

Judith Thurman

Clockface

Hours pass
slowly as a snail
creeping between the grassblades
of the minutes.

Judith Thurman

The Harvest Moon

The flame-red moon, the harvest moon,
Rolls along the hills, gently bouncing,
A vast balloon,
Till it takes off, and sinks upward
To lie in the bottom of the sky, like a gold doubloon.

The harvest moon has come,
Booming softly through heaven, like a bassoon.
And earth replies all night, like a deep drum.

So people can't sleep,
So they go out where elms and oak trees keep
A kneeling vigil, in a religious hush.
The harvest moon has come!

And all the moonlit cows and all the sheep
Stare up at her petrified, while she swells
Filling heaven, as if red hot, and sailing
Closer and closer like the end of the world

Till the gold fields of stiff wheat
Cry 'We are ripe, reap us!' and the rivers
Sweat from the melting hills.

Ted Hughes

Christmas Day

Small girls on trikes
Bigger on bikes
Collars on tykes

Looking like cads
Patterned in plaids
Scarf-wearing dads

Chewing a choc
Mum in a frock
Watches the clock

Knocking in pans
Fetching of grans
Gathering of clans

Hissing from tins
Sherries and gins
Upping of chins

Corks making pops
'Just a few drops'
Watering of chops

All this odd joy
Tears at a broken toy
Just for the birth long ago of a boy

Roy Fuller

The Rabbit's Christmas Carol

I'm sick as a parrot,
I've lost me carrot,
I couldn't care less if it's
Christmas Day.

I'm sick as a parrot,
I've lost me carrot,
So get us a lettuce
Or . . . go away!

Kit Wright

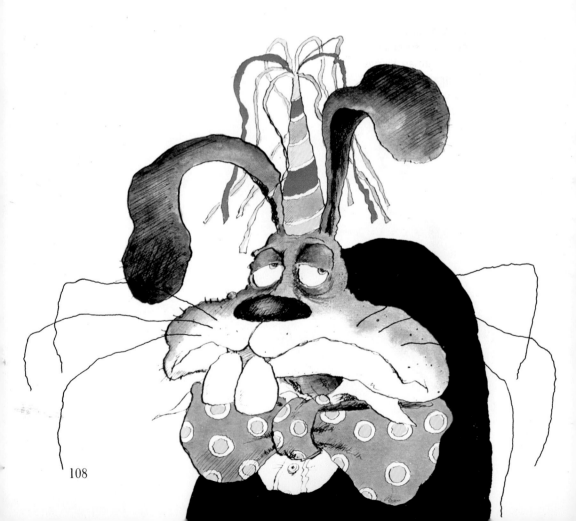

The Turkey

Turkeys don't like Christmas
which may come as no surprise.
They say why don't human beings
pick on people their own size.
To sit beside potatoes
in an oven can't be fun,
so a Turkey is quite justified
to feel he's being done.

Richard Diggance

The Budgie's New Year Message

Get a little tin of bird-seed,
Pour it in my little trough.
If you don't, you little twit, I'll
Bite your little finger off.

Kit Wright

109

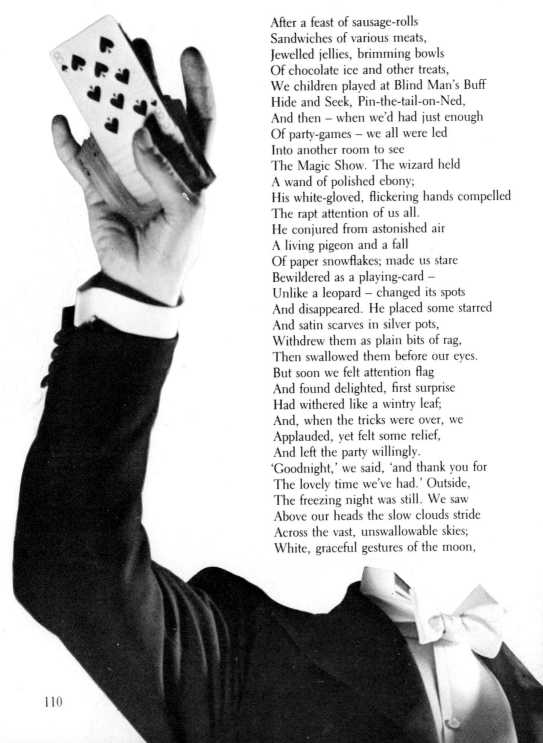

The Magic Show

After a feast of sausage-rolls
Sandwiches of various meats,
Jewelled jellies, brimming bowls
Of chocolate ice and other treats,
We children played at Blind Man's Buff
Hide and Seek, Pin-the-tail-on-Ned,
And then – when we'd had just enough
Of party-games – we all were led
Into another room to see
The Magic Show. The wizard held
A wand of polished ebony;
His white-gloved, flickering hands compelled
The rapt attention of us all.
He conjured from astonished air
A living pigeon and a fall
Of paper snowflakes; made us stare
Bewildered as a playing-card –
Unlike a leopard – changed its spots
And disappeared. He placed some starred
And satin scarves in silver pots,
Withdrew them as plain bits of rag,
Then swallowed them before our eyes.
But soon we felt attention flag
And found delighted, first surprise
Had withered like a wintry leaf;
And, when the tricks were over, we
Applauded, yet felt some relief,
And left the party willingly.
'Goodnight,' we said, 'and thank you for
The lovely time we've had.' Outside,
The freezing night was still. We saw
Above our heads the slow clouds stride
Across the vast, unswallowable skies;
White, graceful gestures of the moon,

The stars' intent and glittering eyes,
And, gleaming like a silver spoon,
The frosty path to lead us home.
Our breath hung blossoms on unseen
Boughs of air as we paused there,
And we forgot that we had been
Pleased briefly by that conjuror,
Could not recall his tricks, or face,
Bewitched and awed, as now we were,
By magic of the common place.

Vernon Scannell

Snow

In the gloom of whiteness,
In the great silence of snow,
A child was sighing
And bitterly saying: 'Oh,
They have killed a white bird up there on her nest,
The down is fluttering from her breast!'
And still it fell through that dusky brightness
On the child crying for the bird of the snow.

Edward Thomas

112

Before a fall

Once upon a sledge a boy called Bill
Hurtled down the chilly paths of snow
That criss-crossed the new surface of a hill
And showed him where his sledge was meant to go.
   But Bill knew best,
    Bill knew better than all the rest;
    Bill decided on his own
     That he would go where no one else had gone.

So up the higher slopes he took his sledge,
Pulled it by the string looped through the front;
Took it to the very topmost edge
Although he heard a voice somewhere say 'don't!'
   For Bill knew best,
    Bill knew better than all the rest;
    Bill reflected on the need
     To teach the other folk the facts of speed.

At many miles an hour he hit the bump
And parted from his sledge (just by the way).
He hit the local snowman with a thump
And thought the starry night had come to stay.
   Still, Bill knew best,
    Bill knew better than all the rest;
    Bill announced, while in his bed,
     He'd MEANT to test the thickness of his head.

Alan Bold

March Snow

It snows again today
And we go out to play
And sledge at the edge
Of the car-stuck road,
Wild and whirling,
Hurling snow cold and hard
From prickling hands,
Watching water trickling
From snow-crammed eaves,
Making an autumn of snowy leaves.
Graves in the churchyard
Lose their cold lead grey
And are warm in the white
Bitter cold that holds them
Gently free from ugly weeds
And decay for a day or two.

And I play with you
In this snow-time.

John Kitching

114

Thaw

Over the land freckled with snow half-thawed
The speculating rooks at their nests cawed
And saw from elm-tops, delicate as flower of grass,
What we below could not see, Winter pass.

Edward Thomas

The Winter Dragon

The wind was scattering flakes of snow
As if it were tearing up the sky
When the hero fastened on his sword
Engraved with spells along both sides.

The snowflakes tumbled over each other
As if they were fleeing in fear
When the hero put his helmet on
And shouldered his long, broad-bladed spear.

Men were bringing the sheep and cattle in
That were freezing to death in the fields
When the hero hung his horn from his neck
And took up his seven-layered shield.

He made his way up the mountain
Through hollows where snowdrifts lay
And over the bare black knuckles of rock
Where the wind had blown the snow away.

And there in a cave on the mountain top
Was the snow-white dragon in its icy hole,
Scaled with ice, bearded with icicles
And breathing out, not flames, but cold.

The hero's shield grew heavy with ice.
He hid from its breath and sounded his horn;
Like shooting flames the blade of his spear
And the blade of his sword began to burn.

The freezing dragon caught fire
And burnt among melting snow;
From the ground that was warmed by its cinders
The Spring flowers began to grow.

Stanley Cook

terry

terry
my tabby-cat
daylong during winter
tattered ears hugged flat
creeps his wily head
closer and closer
to the heaped coal fire
till the flames
singe his fur
bake his belly

later
after I've appealed
to him vainly
to move when I want
to mend the fire
ignoring the names
I call him will yield
like a blob of mercury
to my touch
confident
I'll let him lie I'd rather
let the fire out

when each day
he steps out-
of-doors a bit longer
I know
spring is truly on her way
and when he quits
the house altogether
and sits
trimming and combing his
burnt beard I know
spring has arrived at last

the sun high
he goes to bask
on his back on the path
legs straight and wide
as if tied
bared claws curved to draw
the mouse-warm heat inside
till he begins to purr
and then snore

nap over
rises
lowers his head
stretches
heaps his lean belly
high on his back
becomes for a moment
dromedary
slackens back to cat
grins
licks his chops
flirts
a defiant tail
deliberately skirts
the border biting
off heads of flowers
never dead ones
always the brightest ones

he swaggers as he walks
pleased I'm watching
pleased I'm shaking
my rueful head

stalks slowly to the lilac tree
sits tall egyptian
tigered in leaf light
yearns for the moment when
young birds try their flight
and flutter from the bough
to where he waits below

Albert Rowe

Change

The summer
still hangs
heavy and sweet
with sunlight
as it did last year.

The autumn
still comes
showering gold and crimson
as it did last year.

The winter
still stings
clean and cold and white
as it did last year.

The spring
still comes
like a whisper in the dark night.

It is only I
who have changed.

Charlotte Zolotow

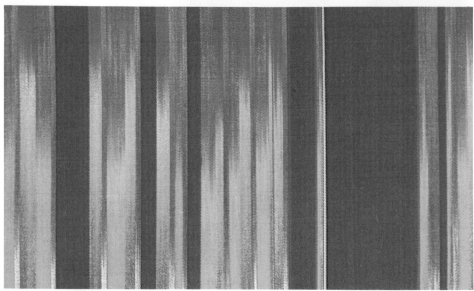

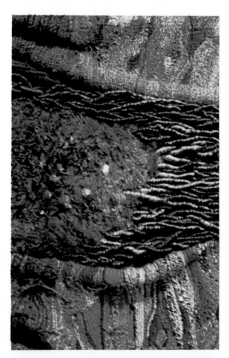

For old times' sake: a tree speaks

I live out my life
in these widening rings
like a thrown stone's ripples
from the centre of things.

I grew with each year
in sunshine and dark;
each ripple expanded
my long coat of bark.

How small my beginnings,
the seed of my heart –
but growing and flowing
with life from the start.

So many bird songs
are caught in my grooves,
and voices, and laughter,
and wild horses' hooves!

I once hid a king
and a highwayman bold;
I've seen thousands of seasons
but don't feel that old.

In winter I'm leafless,
my heart's in my roots.
But when spring comes, the sun
drives new life through my shoots.

I've been struck by the lightning,
been battered by gales;
but through rain, snow and tempest
my faith never fails.

It may be this ring
is the last I shall make,
but I keep the rings turning –
for old times' sake.

James Kirkup

Who

Who is that child I see wandering, wandering
Down by the side of the quivering stream?
Why does he seem not to hear, though I call to him?
Where does he come from, and what is his name?

Why do I see him at sunrise and sunset
Taking, in old-fashioned clothes, the same track?
Why, when he walks, does he cast not a shadow
Though the sun rises and falls at his back?

Why does the dust lie so thick on the hedgerow
By the great field where a horse pulls the plough?
Why do I see only meadows, where houses
Stand in a line by the riverside now?

Why does he move like a wraith by the water,
Soft as the thistledown on the breeze blown?
When I draw near him so that I may hear him,
Why does he say that his name is my own?

Charles Causley

122

After we've gone

Who will live in our house
After we've gone
Will they have green plastic
Instead of a lawn?

Who will live in our house
After the wars?
Will there be mutations
That crawl on all fours?

Will the shiny robot workers
Be dreaming strange, new dreams?
Will the pigeons, big as turkeys
Roost on our ancient beams?

Who will use our kitchen?
What will they cook?
Who will sleep in our room
And how will they look?

Will they feel our ghosts disturbing
Their cybernetic years
With the echoes of our laughter
And the shadows of our tears?

Will there still be lovers?
Who will sing our songs?
Who will live in our house
After we've gone?

Fran Landesman

Index of first lines

Acknowledgements

The following poems are appearing for the first time in this collection and are reprinted by permission of the author unless otherwise stated.

Alan Bold: 'Before a fall'; 'Mary Cummings'; 'John Staffen'; 'A Tail Story' and 'Night Without Light'. All © 1981 Alan Bold. Keith Bosley: 'The Chimney' and 'Ferret'. Both © 1981 Keith Bosley. Gyles Brandreth: 'Animal Chatter', © 1981 Gyles Brandreth. Stanley Cook: 'The Winter Dragon'; 'The Fox Hunt'; 'The Ferry'; 'The Fish'; 'The Convertibles' and 'The Orange Balloon'. All © 1981 Stanley Cook. John Foster: 'War Games', © 1981 John Foster. Roy Fuller: 'Christmas Day', © 1981 Roy Fuller. Gregory Harrison: 'He was a strong but simple man'; 'The Narrow Boats'; 'A Master of Foxhounds' and 'Distracted, the mother said to her boy'. All © 1981 Gregory Harrison. Julie Holder: 'One that got away', © 1981 Julie Holder. James Kirkup: 'For old times' sake: A tree speaks', © 1981 James Kirkup. Reprinted by permission of Dr. Jan Van Loewen Ltd. John Kitching: 'March Snow', © 1981 John Kitching. Wes Magee: 'Tyrannosaurus Rex': 'Rhamphory-nchus' and 'Big Aunt Flo'. All © 1981 Wes Magee. Gareth Owen: 'The Building Site'; and 'My Sister Betty'. Both © 1981 Gareth Owen. Brian Patten: 'The Newcomer'; 'The Love-Doomed Rat'. Both © 1981 Brian Patten. Michael Rosen: 'In the playground', © 1981 Michael Rosen. Albert Rowe: 'Terry', © 1981 Albert Rowe. Vernon Scannell: 'The Magic Show', © 1981 Vernon Scannell. Alan Sillitoe: 'Car Dump' and 'Moth'. Both © 1981 Alan Sillitoe. Iain Crichton Smith: 'On a breezy day'; 'To a Giraffe'; 'Horror Film' and 'The Weasel'. All © 1981 Iain Crichton Smith. Ted Walker: 'The Fight', © 1981 Ted Walker. Reprinted by permission of David Higham Associates Ltd. Raymond Wilson: 'This letter's to say'' and 'Playing Truant'. Both © 1981 Raymond Wilson.

The Editor and Publisher wish to thank the following for permission to reprint copyright poems in this anthology:

Dannie Abse: 'Emperors of the Island' from *Collected Poems 1948–1976* (Hutchinson 1977). Reprinted by permission of Anthony Sheil Associates Ltd. N. M. Bodecker: 'An Explorer Named Bliss' from *A Person From Britain Whose Head Was the Shape of a Mitten & Other Limericks*. Copyright © 1980 by N. M. Bodecker. A Margaret K. McElderry book (New York: Atheneum 1980/Dent, 1980). Reprinted by permission of, J. M. Dent & Sons Ltd., and Atheneum Publishers. Alan Brownjohn: 'Parrot' and 'Chameleon', from *Brownjohn's Beasts*.